Somatic Healing for Beginners

25+ Simple Ways to Relieve Trauma, Tension, and Anxiety in 15 Minutes a Day.

EMLIK. SAHRA

EMLIK. SAHRA

Somatic Healing for Beginners

Contents

EMLIK. SAHRA

Somatic Healing for Beginners

EMLIK. SAHRA

INTRODUCTION

Understanding Somatic Healing

Many of us suffer with unseen burdens such as stress, anxiety, and trauma in today's fast-paced environment full of constant pressures and distractions. These experiences can build up inside of us, manifesting not only in our bodies but also our minds. Allow me to present somatic healing, a powerful practice that recognizes the significant relationship between the mind and body and allows us to treat emotional and psychological traumas at their source.

The insight that our bodies are more than merely vehicles for our minds is the cornerstone of somatic healing. Rather, they are living, breathing things that store our memories, emotions, and traumas. Consider your body to be a diary, with each discomfort, pain, and tension having a story to share. Somatic healing urges us to pay attention to our bodily experiences since it recognizes them as avenues for healing.

This strategy tries to strengthen our bond with ourselves rather than simply treating symptoms. Learning to tune into our body feelings allows us to uncover the layers of stress and trauma that have taken up residence within us. Releasing these weights through somatic healing allows us to restore harmony and balance in our lives in a gentle yet effective manner.

EMLIK. SAHRA

Relationship Between Mind and Body

The mind-body link is not a new concept; it has long been recognized in many healing traditions and cultures. However, modern science has begun to catch up, providing a multitude of evidence that supports the premise that our mental feelings have a big impact on our physical well-being.

Consider how stress affects you physically. You may experience a racing heart, stomach cramps, or shoulder discomfort. These bodily reactions are the body's way of communicating pain, and they are more than merely reactions. Somatic healing encourages us to decipher these signals and recognize that our emotions are not separate from our physical selves, but rather fundamental to our overall well-being.

Trauma, whether caused by a single stressful event or a series of stresses, can cause our bodies to become tight and protective. This is the ideal place for somatic recovery. We can free ourselves from the behaviors that hold us back and allow for healing and renewal by engaging in techniques that promote body awareness and release.

We learn that healing is a holistic process as we study the mind-body connection. It requires paying attention to our feelings, thoughts, and physical sensations all at the same time. This comprehensive strategy can be navigated with the help of somatic healing, which promotes the development of a deeper understanding of oneself and experience.

EMLIK. SAHRA

How This Book Works: A 15-Minute Daily Schedule

It's conceivable you're wondering how somatic healing fits into your busy schedule. The good news is that each chapter of this book focuses on simple tactics that you can implement in as little as 15 minutes per day. It is intended to be an approachable and practical handbook. It can make a significant difference to take a moment to concentrate oneself in our fast-paced world.

Each chapter describes a specific approach or exercise for releasing tension, anxiety, and trauma. These practices, which include breathing exercises, grounding exercises, and gentle movements, were created with beginners in mind and need no time or equipment. All you need is a willingness to research and connect with your body; no specific environment or extensive training is required.

To help you along your journey, we've included practice summaries, short advice, and personal experiences throughout the book. These components will help you stay motivated and involved throughout your rehabilitation journey. There are also recommendations and reflections to help you gain more self-awareness and understanding.

As you embark on this journey, remember that rehabilitation is not a straight line. It unfolds differently for each person, and it is critical to be patient and kind with oneself. Allow the activities in this book to serve as a springboard for a more in-depth relationship with your body and emotions.

EMLIK. SAHRA

Somatic Healing for Beginners

Are you ready to start now? The next pages contain over twenty-five simple strategies for relieving tension, anxiety, and trauma while creating a better bond with your body. Let's embark on this life-changing journey to uncover the power of somatic healing and reclaim the vitality and tranquility that are naturally yours.

EMLIK. SAHRA

(Chapter 1:)

Somatic Healing Foundations

1.1 Somatic Healing: What is it?

Somatic healing integrates the mind and body, acknowledging the strong relationship between our physical, emotional, and psychological experiences. The term "somatic" comes from the Greek word "soma," which meaning "body." Fundamentally, somatic healing encourages us to reconnect with our physical selves and acknowledges the powerful influence our bodies have on our mental and emotional wellbeing.

Many people in today's society have perfected the technique of compartmentalizing their experiences. We commonly consider our bodies and thoughts to be separate, which can result in detachment and persistent tension, anxiety, and unresolved trauma. To overcome this alienation, somatic healing promotes awareness of our physical feelings, thoughts, and behaviors.

Consider this: When was the last time you felt stressed? How did your body respond? Maybe your breathing became shallower, your shoulders tensed, or your chest felt constricted. These reactions are more than just physical; they

EMLIK. SAHRA

also communicate emotions. Somatic healing helps us communicate with our bodies and minds by teaching us how to recognize these signs.

The beauty of somatic healing is in its simplicity. It does not necessitate much training or elaborate ceremonies. Instead, it encourages us to engage in techniques that foster awareness and release. Breathwork, gentle movement, and mindfulness exercises are examples of approaches that can help us gain a better knowledge of our bodies and the emotions they contain.

In essence, somatic healing is about recovering our natural ability to heal. Recognizing that our bodies contain knowledge allows us to begin exploring and addressing the underlying reasons of our misery, paving the door for significant transformation.

1.2 The Science of Somatic Practices

The convergence of science and somatic healing presents an intriguing world of knowledge. Researchers and practitioners have begun to identify the physiological and psychological principles underlying somatic practices, giving solid evidence for their efficacy.

The autonomic nerve system (ANS) is a key topic in somatic healing since it regulates our involuntary biological activities such as heart rate, digestion, and breathing rate. The ANS is separated into two parts: the sympathetic nervous system (SNS) and the parasympathetic nervous system (PNS). The SNS controls our fight-or-flight response, which is activated when we perceive a threat. In contrast, the PNS produces a sense of calm and relaxation.

When we are subjected to trauma or persistent stress, our bodies may become locked in sympathetic activation. This prolonged activation can cause a variety of medical and psychological difficulties, including anxiety, sadness, and chronic pain. Somatic healing therapies seek to engage the PNS, allowing a transition from a state of survival to one of safety and relaxation.

Deep breathing, mindfulness meditation, and mild movement have all been demonstrated to have a favorable impact on the ANS. For example, studies have shown that deep, diaphragmatic breathing activates the PNS, increasing relaxation and lowering anxiety levels. Similarly, mindfulness activities have been shown to reduce cortisol levels, a hormone linked to stress.

Furthermore, the importance of bodily awareness in somatic healing cannot be overemphasized. According to research, people who become more aware of their body feelings have less anxiety and better emotional regulation. Somatic healing allows people to recognize and release bodily manifestations of emotional suffering, enhancing overall well-being.

Furthermore, polyvagal theory, created by Dr. Stephen Porges, provides insights into how our physiological reactions are linked to our emotional moods. According to this hypothesis, our bodies have inbuilt systems for social interaction, safety, and connection. Somatic activities that encourage relaxation and awareness can engage these systems, creating a sense of safety and connection that is necessary for healing.

Somatic Healing for Beginners

In conclusion, the study of somatic practices gives a strong framework for understanding how our bodies and thoughts interact. By engaging with our physical sensations and using relaxation techniques, we can access our intrinsic healing power, paving the road for emotional and psychological well-being.

1.3 Advantages of Somatic Healing for Trauma and Anxiety

Somatic healing has benefits that are as diverse as the people who practice it. Whether you are dealing with the consequences of trauma, anxiety, or simply seeking a deeper connection with oneself, somatic healing has a wide range of transforming benefits.

One of the key advantages of somatic healing is its capacity to address trauma at its source. Traditional therapeutic approaches frequently concentrate on cognitive processes, enabling people to express their thoughts and feelings. While this is useful, it does not always account for the physical manifestations of trauma in the body. Somatic healing bridges this gap by enabling people to examine and release the sensations that come with their experiences.

Individuals who engage in somatic techniques can process trauma in a safe and supportive setting. For example, gentle movements and breathwork can help to release pent-up energy and stress, allowing for a cathartic release. This approach frequently results in a tremendous sense of relief and liberation, allowing people to rediscover their sense of self and agency.

Furthermore, somatic healing has been demonstrated to be particularly useful in the treatment of anxiety. Somatic practices use strategies to regulate the nervous system, which promotes a sense of peace and safety. Many people report that including somatic techniques into their everyday routines greatly reduces anxiety and increases overall emotional resilience.

Furthermore, the benefits of somatic healing go beyond the immediate reduction of trauma and anxiety. Individuals who engage in these routines frequently report feeling more self-aware and mindful. This enhanced awareness allows them to recognize and handle triggers, resulting in more effective coping techniques in the face of stress.

Somatic healing has another big advantage: it is easily accessible. The methods presented in this book are simple to implement and need only a few minutes of focused time each day. Whether you're at home, at work, or in a public place, somatic practices can help you reconnect with your body and decrease stress.

Furthermore, somatic healing promotes a feeling of empowerment. As people learn to listen to their bodies and respond to their needs, they develop a stronger bond with themselves. This self-empowerment is revolutionary, allowing people to reclaim their stories and actively pursue healing and progress.

Finally, the communal aspect of somatic healing cannot be disregarded. Many people feel that engaging in somatic techniques in a supportive environment improves their experience. Whether through seminars, group sessions, or shared practices with friends, a sense of connection and support can increase the advantages of somatic therapy, creating a shared space for growth and recovery.

Finally, the foundations of somatic healing offer a rich tapestry of understanding that connects body, mind, and spirit. As we explore the different practices and techniques in this book, you will learn how to use the power of somatic healing to alleviate trauma, tension, and anxiety in your life. Accept this trip with an open heart and mind, and allow yourself to feel the transformational power of reconnecting with your body and emotions.

EMLIK. SAHRA

(Chapter 2:)

Preparing for Your Journey

2.1 Set Up Your Space

Creating a dedicated place for your somatic healing practice is an important step toward creating a caring atmosphere in which to connect with yourself on a deeper level. Your space should feel safe, inviting, and relaxing. This chapter will lead you through the process of creating an environment that aligns with your recovery path.

Choosing the Right Location.

The first step in creating your healing area is to choose a suitable location. It does not have to be a large space; a corner of a room, a cozy nook, or even a piece in your garden can serve as your sanctuary. The idea is to find a place where you feel at ease and devoid of distractions. Ideally, this setting should be quiet, allowing you to concentrate on your workout without distractions.

Decluttering and Organizing

EMLIK. SAHRA

Somatic Healing for Beginners

Once you've decided on a location, it's time to clean up and organize. A clutter-free atmosphere increases mental clarity and your ability to relax. Remove any objects that do not support your goal or provide distractions. This may include unnecessary furnishings, electronics, or anything that causes tension. Consider keeping those items that inspire you or contribute positively to your healing process.

Creating a Calming Environment.

Now that you've decluttered, consider how to create a relaxing atmosphere. Consider the elements listed below:

Lighting: If natural light is unavailable, use warm, soothing lighting instead. Dimmer switches and soft lights can help to create a pleasant atmosphere. Candles are another excellent option, as they induce relaxation and provide a peaceful glow.

Colors: Choose colors that have personal importance for you. Earth tones, blues, and greens are examples of soft, muted colors that are thought to have a soothing effect. These colors are suitable for use in paintings, fabrics, and other types of artworks.

Textures: To create a sensory-rich atmosphere, use a range of textures in your area. Adding plush carpets, cushions, and blankets to your room can improve its comfort. Use organic materials such as stone or wood to deepen your connection with nature.

Somatic Healing for Beginners

Scent: Aromatherapy has a significant impact on your emotional health. Think about using fragrant candles, incense, or essential oils. Aromas like eucalyptus, chamomile, and lavender may help with grounding and relaxation.

Sound: Using sound in your healing process may be really beneficial. Create a playlist of relaxing meditations, nature sounds, or music to listen to while training. Instead, consider augmenting your experience with sound bowls or mild chimes.

Individual touches.

Finally, provide sentimental elements that appeal to you. Examples include nostalgic items, plants that brighten your space, and motivating artwork. Crystals, mantras, and images of your loved ones can all help to boost your atmosphere. Remember that this space is entirely yours; it serves as a haven for your therapeutic activities and a reflection of your path.

2.2 Attitude and Goals.

Before you begin your somatic healing journey, you must have the right mindset and set clear intentions. Your perspective will shape your experience by choosing how you interact with the exercises and your openness to the healing process.

Developing a Growth Mindset.

Somatic Healing for Beginners

Approaching somatic healing with an open heart necessitates a growth mindset. This way of thinking embraces the idea that healing is a process and that all experiences, good or terrible, help you grow. It encourages you to perceive setbacks as opportunities to improve rather than obstacles.

Recognize any concerns or assumptions you may have about how the healing process will begin. It is normal to feel uneasy, especially if you are enduring trauma or worry. Instead of allowing these feelings to keep you back, use them as stepping stones to your growth. Accept that hurdles are a regular part of the journey and that healing is a non-linear process.

Setting Goals for Your Work

Setting intentions offers your healing process structure and direction. An intention is a guiding principle that aligns your focus and energy, not just a goal. When you set an intention, you are effectively expressing your commitment to your healing process and bringing positive change into your life.

To set your intentions, consider your somatic healing goals. Consider the following inquiries.

Which aspects of my life do I want to focus on?
How would I like my body and mind to feel?
What kind of changes do I want to make in my life?
Once you've made your intentions clear, write them down on paper. This gesture indicates your dedication and serves as a continual reminder during the

Somatic Healing for Beginners

duration of your journey. As you progress, you may elect to review and adjust your goals so that they evolve alongside you.

Application of Presence and Mindfulness

Developing a development mentality, setting intentions, and engaging in mindfulness practices are all necessary for maximizing your somatic healing process. The art of mindfulness is to be present in the moment without passing judgment. It invites you to give curious and caring attention to your ideas, emotions, and bodily sensations.

To begin practicing mindfulness, concentrate on your breathing. Spend a few minutes each day just breathing and focusing on the rhythm of your own breath. Consider how your body feels after each breath and expiration. This practice will help you become more aware of your body and emotions, paving the door for deeper healing.

Embracing self-compassion

Finally, practice self-compassion throughout your journey. Healing can be difficult, and it's easy to fall into a cycle of self-criticism when progress seems slow. Remind yourself that healing is a process, and it's normal to feel a variety of emotions along the way.

Practice self-kindness by speaking to yourself as you would to a close friend. Recognize your efforts, praise your accomplishments, and allow yourself to

Somatic Healing for Beginners

experience whatever emotions occur without judgment. Cultivating a caring mindset provides a solid basis for your healing path.

As you prepare to engage in somatic healing activities, having the correct tools and materials might improve your experience. While your body and breath are the key instruments for somatic healing, external resources can provide support and guidance as you embark on this path.

Essential Tools for Somatic Healing

Wear loose, comfortable clothes that allows for free movement during practice. This allows you to fully engage with your body without limits.

A yoga mat or soft blanket can serve as a pleasant platform for lying down or sitting throughout your practices. It provides a specific location for your somatic work, allowing you to feel grounded.

A journal can be an effective instrument for self-reflection and exploration. Use it to jot down your ideas, feelings, and insights as you proceed through your recovery process. You might also write down your aims and any observations that arise during your practices.

Somatic Healing for Beginners

Meditation Cushion or Chair: If you like to sit throughout your activities, you can use a meditation cushion or a comfortable chair. This will help you keep a comfortable posture while doing mindfulness or other somatic exercises.
Sound Instruments: If you enjoy sound healing, consider adding singing bowls, chimes, or a quiet music player to your room. These noises can enhance your experience by allowing you to relax and connect with your body.

Aromatherapy: Essential oils can be an effective technique for generating a tranquil environment. Choose essential oils that appeal to you, such as lavender for relaxation or citrus for upliftment. Use a diffuser or apply a drop on your wrists before beginning your practice.

Recommended Resources:

Explore books about somatic healing, mindfulness, and trauma recovery. Some highly suggested titles include "The Body Keeps the Score" by Bessel van der Kolk, "Waking the Tiger" by Peter Levine, and "Somatic Experiencing" by Levine.

Consider taking online classes or attending workshops on somatic practices. These tools frequently give structured assistance and community support, which improves your learning experience.

Mobile Apps: There are various meditation and mindfulness apps available to help you practice. Apps such as Insight Timer, Calm, and Headspace provide guided meditations, breathing exercises, and soundscapes to help you heal.

Somatic Healing for Beginners

YouTube and Podcasts: Discover videos and podcasts about somatic healing and mindfulness. Many practitioners provide useful insights, guided practices, and discussions to inspire and motivate you on your journey.

Support Groups and Communities: Look for support groups or online communities dedicated to somatic healing or trauma recovery. Connecting with others who have had similar experiences can bring a sense of belonging and encouragement.

Therapists and Coaches: If you believe it might be beneficial, consult with a therapist or coach who specializes in somatic healing. Their knowledge can help you manage your path with individualized coaching.

Call to action

Appreciate you reading! I would want to take a moment to personally thank you for selecting to read my work. Your time and effort are much valued; perhaps, this book will give you insightful analysis and successful techniques.

Your comments are very much valued as I develop as an author. I would love to hear your thoughts—whether positive or constructive—so I can improve and make future works even more helpful and engaging.

 I respectfully ask that you write an honest review whether you thought this book was beneficial or if you could see anything improved. Your observations will not only help me but also guide other readers toward appropriate materials.

I appreciate your support once more; I am looking forward your comments. Good wishes,

EMLIK. SAHRA

(Chapter 3:)

Breathing Techniques.

Breathing is one of the most effective yet neglected methods for dealing with stress, anxiety, and emotional turbulence. It's something we do intuitively, but when used intentionally, it can serve as a gateway to significant physical recovery. In this chapter, we'll look at three fundamental breathing techniques: diaphragmatic breathing, box breathing, and the 4-7-8 Breathing Technique. Each of these strategies has distinct benefits and can be implemented in a matter of minutes, making them ideal for your daily routine.

3.1 Diaphragmatic Breathing.

What is Diaphragmatic Breathing?

Diaphragmatic breathing, often known as abdominal or belly breathing, entails fully contracting the diaphragm while inhaling. This approach encourages deeper breathing and improves oxygen exchange, which can help alleviate stress and anxiety. Allowing your diaphragm to descend more fully promotes more air intake, resulting in greater relaxation and tranquility.

Somatic Healing for Beginners

How to Practice Diaphragmatic Breathing

Find Your Space: Begin by deciding on a comfortable position. You can sit in a chair with your feet flat on the floor or lie down on your back. If you're lying down, place a pillow under your knees to reduce lower back stiffness.

Position Your Hands: To feel your breath, place one on your chest and the other on your abdomen. This will allow you to distinguish between shallow chest breathing and deeper diaphragmatic breathing.

Inhale Slowly: Close your eyes and inhale slowly and deeply through your nose. Allow your abdomen to lift as your diaphragm descends during inhalation. Try to keep your chest fairly steady.

Exhale Gently: Slowly exhale through your mouth or nose, allowing your abdomen to sink as you release the air. Try to make your exhalation longer than your inhalation.

Continue the Cycle: Repeat this technique for many minutes, concentrating on the rise and fall of your abdomen. If your mind wanders, softly return your attention to your breathing.

Benefits of Diaphragmatic Breathing

Regularly practicing diaphragmatic breathing can provide numerous benefits, including:

Somatic Healing for Beginners

Reduced Stress and Anxiety: By activating the relaxation response, this approach can help lower cortisol levels and relieve tension.

Improved Oxygen Delivery: Better oxygen exchange can lead to more energy and mental clarity.

Improved Emotional Regulation: Diaphragmatic breathing can help you handle overwhelming emotions and gain a sense of control.

Improved Physical Health: Regular practice can result in reduced blood pressure, better digestion, and stronger immune function.

Integrating Diaphragmatic Breathing into Daily Life

To get the benefits of diaphragmatic breathing, incorporate it into your everyday practice. You might begin your day with a few minutes of this technique, use it during stressful times, or relax before bed. It's a handy tool that will help you stay grounded and mindful throughout the day.

3.2 Box Breathing.

What is Box Breathing?

Box breathing, also called square breathing, is an organized breathing technique that consists of four equal parts: inhalation, holding the breath, exhalation, and another hold. This technique is popular among sportsmen and military personnel because it improves focus and relaxes the nervous system.

How to Practice Box Breathing.

Get Comfortable: Sit in a comfortable position, with your back straight and your shoulders relaxed.

Inhale: Take a deep breath through your nose for four counts, allowing your abdomen to rise.

Gently hold your breath for a count of four. Use this moment to focus on the peace and tranquility that comes with this pause.

Exhale: Slowly exhale through your lips for four counts, allowing your abdomen to descend as you release the air.

Hold Again: Hold your breath for a count of four before repeating the cycle.

Repeat this method for a few rounds, progressively increasing the duration as you gain confidence in the technique.

Benefits of Box Breathing

Box breathing has various benefits, making it a wonderful addition to your somatic healing toolbox.

Somatic Healing for Beginners

Increased Focus and Clarity: Because this technique is structured, it can help you focus more effectively, which is especially useful before difficult activities.

Enhanced Relaxation: The rhythm of box breathing activates the parasympathetic nerve system, which promotes relaxation and reduces anxiety.

Emotional Balance: By generating a pause between inhalation and exhale, box breathing allows you to regulate your emotional responses, promoting calm.

Physical Benefits: Consistent practice can enhance lung capacity and cardiovascular health, as well as a general sense of well-being.

Implementing Box Breathing in Your Routine

Box breathing can be done anywhere, including your workstation, a waiting area, or even during a difficult situation at home. Consider incorporating it into your regular schedule, perhaps as a centering practice before meals or meetings. Its systematic approach makes it an effective tool for mindfulness and stress reduction.

3.3 Breathing Technique (4-7-8)

What is the 4-7-8 breathing technique?

Dr. Andrew Weil developed the 4-7-8 breathing technique to promote relaxation and anxiety management. This approach consists of breathing for four counts, holding for seven counts, then exhaling for eight counts. The longer exhale triggers the body's relaxation response, making it an effective tool for soothing both the mind and body.

How to Use the 4-7-8 Breathing Technique

Find Your Position: Sit or lie down in a comfortable position, with your back straight.

Close Your Eyes: Gently close your eyes to reduce distractions and direct your attention inward.

Inhale gently through your nose for a count of four.

Hold your breath for a count of seven. During this time, concentrate on the quiet within yourself.

Exhale: For a count of eight, exhale completely through your mouth, releasing the air with a whooshing sound.

Repeat to finish one cycle. Begin with four cycles and progressively go to eight as you get more familiar with the method.

Advantages of the 4-7-8 Breathing Technique.

The 4-7-8 breathing technique has various advantages that improve your general well-being:

EMLIK. SAHRA

Rapid Relaxation: This approach can swiftly relax a hyperactive mind, making it ideal for bedtime or stressful situations.

Reduced Anxiety: By controlling your breathing, you can reduce anxiety and achieve a sensation of calm.

Improved Sleep Quality: Regular practice can enhance your ability to fall asleep, calming racing thoughts and promoting deeper sleep.

Focusing on the rhythm of your breath promotes mindfulness and present-moment awareness.

Integrating 4-7-8 Breathing into Your Life.

Consider incorporating the 4-7-8 approach into your sleep routine to indicate to your body that it is time to relax. You can also practice it in high-stress situations, such as before a presentation or when you're feeling overwhelmed. With practice, this approach can become a dependable tool for reaching peace and clarity.

Mastering these breathing techniques—Diaphragmatic Breathing, Box Breathing, and the 4-7-8 Breathing Technique—will help you manage stress, anxiety, and emotional tension successfully. Keep in mind that consistency is essential when implementing these principles. The more you incorporate them into your everyday routine, the greater their impact on your general well-being. As we continue our journey through somatic healing, these breathing techniques will serve as basic tools that can be smoothly integrated into the other practices we will cover in subsequent chapters. Accept the power of your breath and let it led you to a deeper connection with yourself.

(Chapter 4:)

Grounding Exercises.

In our fast-paced, often hectic lives, it's easy to lose touch with ourselves and the current moment. Grounding activities are an effective approach to reconnect with ourselves, promoting a sense of stability and peace in the midst of noise. In this chapter, we'll look at three transformative grounding practices: body scan meditation, grounding visualization, and nature walks for grounding. Each method encourages you to immerse yourself in the present moment, which can help you relieve stress, anxiety, and trauma.

4.1 Body Scan Meditation.

What is body scan meditation?

Body Scan Meditation is a mindfulness practice that promotes awareness of physical sensations all over the body. By systematically focusing your attention on various bodily areas, you can develop a stronger connection with yourself, relieve stress, and encourage relaxation. This technique is especially useful for people who suffer from anxiety or feel disconnected from their bodies.

How To Practice Body Scan Meditation

Somatic Healing for Beginners

Find a Quiet Space: Begin by selecting a peaceful setting where you will not be interrupted. You can either recline on a yoga mat or sit comfortably on a chair.

Get Comfortable: If you're lying down, gently rest your arms by your sides. If sitting, keep your feet flat on the ground and your back straight.

Close Your Eyes: Gently close your eyes to reduce distractions and direct your attention inward.

Take a few deep diaphragmatic breaths to center yourself. Inhale deeply through your nose, allowing your abdomen to rise, then gently exhale through your mouth.

Start with Your Head: Bring your attention to the top of your head. Observe any sensations, tensions, or tightness. Simply watch without judgment.

Shift Your Focus Downward: Begin with your forehead, then your eyes, cheeks, and jaw. Spend a few moments focusing on each location, noticing any feelings or emotions that arise.

Continue the Journey: Move down your body, concentrating on your neck, shoulders, arms, chest, belly, back, hips, legs, and feet. Take a moment with each body part, breathing into any points of tension or discomfort.

Somatic Healing for Beginners

Reconnect and Reflect: After scanning your entire body, take a time to breathe deeply and observe how you feel. Allow yourself to be present, taking in the sensations of relaxation and alertness.

Benefits of Body Scan Meditation.

Incorporating Body Scan Meditation into your regimen can give numerous benefits.

Enhanced Body Awareness: This technique encourages a stronger connection with your body, allowing you to notice tension and stress patterns.

Body scans can help reduce anxiety and stress by encouraging relaxation and mindfulness.

Emotional Release: Allowing oneself to feel and accept bodily feelings helps promote emotional healing and release.

Improved Sleep: Consistent practice can help to calm the mind and prepare the body for restful sleep.

Integrating Body Scan Meditation into Everyday Life

Consider dedicating time each day to a Body Scan Meditation, whether in the morning to establish a positive tone for the day or at night to decompress before bed. Shorter variations can also be used throughout the day to relieve stress and tension.

4.2 Grounding Visualization

What is Grounding Visualization?

Grounding Visualization is a mental activity that allows you to connect with the earth and stay in the present moment. You can use visualization to establish a sense of safety and stability, which will effectively soothe your mind and body. This strategy is especially useful when you're feeling overwhelmed or detached.

How to Practice Grounding Visualization.

Choose Your Space: Locate a peaceful and comfortable area where you may sit or lie down without interruption.

Close Your Eyes: Gently close your eyes to reduce distractions and direct your focus inward.

Take a few deep breaths to focus yourself. Inhale with your nose and exhale through your mouth.

Visualize Roots: Imagine roots growing from the soles of your feet into the ground. Imagine them growing deeper and deeper, securely holding you to the ground.

EMLIK. SAHRA

Somatic Healing for Beginners

Feel the Connection: As you breathe, envision the earth's energy coming up via these roots, filling your body with warmth and solidity. Allow yourself to feel linked to the ground below you.

Engage Your Senses: As you envision, use your senses. What do the roots feel like? Can you hear the earth around you? Imagine the ground's colors and textures.

Stay Present: Stay in this visualization for a few minutes, allowing the sense of grounding and safety to wash over you. If your thoughts wander, gently return your attention to the image of the roots.

Return Gradually: When you're ready, bring your attention back to the present moment. Take a few long breaths before gradually opening your eyes.

Advantages of Grounding Visualization

Grounding Visualization has a number of advantages that can boost your general well-being:

Increased Calm and Clarity: This approach reduces anxiety, helping you to refocus and concentrate.

Sense of Safety: Visualizing a connection to the soil increases emotions of security, allowing you to feel more grounded in difficult times.

Somatic Healing for Beginners

Emotional Regulation: Anchoring yourself in the present moment allows you to better control overpowering emotions.

Grounding Visualization can promote creative thinking by establishing a serene mental environment.

Integrating Grounding Visualization into Your Routine

You can use Grounding Visualization whenever you want to reconnect with your body and the present moment. Consider utilizing it on stressful workdays, prior to critical meetings, or as part of your morning or evening ritual.

4.3 Nature Walks for Grounding.

What is a Nature Walk for Grounding?

Nature walks are an effective grounding activity that links you with the natural world. Being in outdoors can relieve stress, improve mood, and build a strong connection to the land. Immersing yourself in nature, whether through a park, forest, or beach, may be therapeutic and rejuvenating.

How to Conduct Nature Walks for Grounding

Choose Your Location: Select a natural setting that appeals to you. This might be a neighborhood park, a hiking trail, or any other outdoor area where you can feel the ground beneath your feet.

Somatic Healing for Beginners

Prepare Yourself: Before you start walking, take a moment to center yourself. Stand motionless, close your eyes, and take a few deep breaths to center yourself in the present now.

Engage Your Senses: As you begin walking, pay attention to your surroundings. Take in the colors, sounds, and textures around you. Feel the ground under your feet and the air against your skin.

Practice Mindful Walking: With each step, concentrate on the feelings in your body. Feel the movement of your legs and arms, the rhythm of your breath, and the sensation of your feet on the ground.

Embrace Nature: Allow yourself to be completely present in the event. Observe the trees, flowers, and wildlife. Listen to the sounds of nature, such as rustling leaves, chirping birds, and the calm flow of water.

Pause & Reflect: Find an area that speaks to you and pause for a moment. Take a deep breath and reflect on your feelings. Allow the beauty and serenity of nature to sweep over you.

Conclude Mindfully: After your walk, take a time to express your gratitude for the experience. Recognize any fluctuations in your mood or energy levels.

Advantages of Nature Walks for Grounding

Participating in nature walks provides numerous benefits:

Somatic Healing for Beginners

Stress Reduction: Studies have shown that being in nature lowers cortisol levels, promoting relaxation and lowering anxiety.

Improved Mood: Spending time in nature can improve your mood and make you feel more relaxed.

Walking is an excellent form of exercise for improving cardiovascular health and overall fitness.

Nature walks are an excellent opportunity for mindfulness practice, as they allow you to be present and fully engaged in the moment.

Integrating Nature Walks into Your Routine

To incorporate nature walks into your routine, set aside time each week to explore nearby parks or trails. You can also turn these walks into a social activity by inviting friends or family to accompany you. Even a short walk during your lunch break can help you regain energy and improve your overall health.

Grounding exercises are essential for reconnecting with yourself and the present moment. Body Scan Meditation, Grounding Visualization, and Nature Walks can help you achieve a state of stability and calm that will nourish your mind, body, and spirit. These practices not only reduce stress and anxiety, but they also foster a stronger connection with your body and the world around you.

EMLIK. SAHRA

(Chapter 5:)

Movement Practices.

Movement is one of the most effective methods for releasing tension, trauma, and anxiety stored in the body. In this chapter, we will explore three transforming movement practices: Gentle Stretching Routines, Somatic Movements for Release, and Dance as a Healing Tool. Each of these activities invites you to connect with your body in a loving and mindful way, supporting healing and resilience.

5.1 Gentle Stretching Routines

What Are Gentle Stretching Routines?

Gentle stretching techniques are designed to enhance relaxation and flexibility while developing awareness of the body. Unlike intensive workouts, these routines prioritize listening to your body's demands, helping you to release physical and mental strain. Gentle stretches can be practiced at any time of day, making them an accessible tool for everyone, regardless of fitness level.

How to Practice Gentle Stretching

EMLIK. SAHRA

Somatic Healing for Beginners

Create a Comfortable Environment: Choose a quiet location where you may stretch without distractions. You might want to use a yoga mat or a soft surface to guarantee comfort.

Warm Up with Deep Breathing: Before you begin stretching, take a few moments to center yourself with deep, diaphragmatic breaths. Inhale through your nose, expanding your abdomen, and exhale through your mouth, releasing any tension.

Start with the Neck: Gently lower your chin to your chest and move your head from side to side. Take your time, allowing each movement to feel peaceful. This easy stretch eases neck strain and promotes relaxation.

Shoulder Rolls: Raise your shoulders to your ears and roll them back and forth in a circular motion. Repeat a few times to relieve tension in the shoulders and upper back.

Side Stretch: Sit or stand comfortably. Reach one arm overhead and lean to the opposite side, feeling the stretch on your side. Hold for a few breaths and then switch sides.

Cat-Cow Stretch: If you're at ease on your hands and knees, alternate between arching your back (cat stance) and lowering your belly to the ground. This stretch relieves tension in the spine and enhances flexibility.

Seated Forward Bend: Sit with your legs stretched out in front of you. Inhale to stretch your spine, then exhale as you slowly lean forward, reaching for your toes or shins. Hold for a few breaths to feel the stretch in your hamstrings and lower back.

Child's Pose: Finish your stretching regimen with Child's Pose. Kneel on the ground, sit back on your heels, and extend your arms forward, resting your forehead on the mat. This pose promotes calm and surrender.

Benefits of Gentle Stretching.

Adding mild stretching to your regimen can have various benefits:

Increased Flexibility: Stretching on a regular basis improves range of motion and flexibility, making daily activities easier and more pleasant.

Reduced Muscle Tension: Stretching helps to release physical tension stored in the muscles, resulting in relaxation and comfort.

Gentle stretching promotes body awareness and a stronger connection with your physical self.

Stretching improves circulation by increasing blood flow to the muscles, which promotes general health and vigor.

Incorporating Gentle Stretching into Your Routine

EMLIK. SAHRA

Somatic Healing for Beginners

Consider incorporating mild stretching into your regular routine by setting aside time each morning or evening. You can also incorporate small stretching breaks throughout the day, especially if you spend a lot of time sitting down.

5.2 Somatic Movements to Release

What Are the Somatic Movements for Release?

Somatic movements are deliberate, conscious movements that increase awareness of body feelings and emotions. Unlike typical exercise, somatic movements focus on the interior experience, allowing you to access your body's wisdom for healing and release. This practice helps you to move in a way that feels wonderful, encouraging both mental and physical well-being.

How to Practice Somatic Movement for Release

Create a Safe Space: Locate a peaceful, comfortable space where you can move freely and without interruption. This area should feel safe and welcoming.

Tune In to Your Body: Start by standing or sitting comfortably. Close your eyes and take a few deep breaths, focusing on the feelings in your body. Take note of any moments of tension, discomfort, or emotion that arise.

Start with Gentle Movement: Move your body in any way that feels natural. This could include swaying from side to side, rotating your hips, or lightly shaking your arms. Allow your body to guide the way while trusting your intuition.

Somatic Healing for Beginners

Focus on Sensations: As you move, pay attention to how your body feels. Notice where you have tightness or discomfort and let yourself to move in a way that promotes release.

Experiment with different movements, like stretching, twisting, and bending. Follow your body's cues and let go of any expectations or judgments.

Allow yourself to physically express any feelings that occur during your movement exercise. This could include vocalizing, exercising more forcefully, or finding silence to absorb your emotions.

Conclude with Stillness: After several minutes of movement, return to a state of stillness. Stand or sit calmly, allowing yourself to experience the benefits of the activity. Take a few deep breaths and notice if anything changes in your body or thoughts.

Benefits of Somatic Movement for Release

Practicing somatic movements can have great advantages.

Emotional Release: Somatic movements help you release pent-up emotions and promote emotional healing.

Increased Body Awareness: This practice raises your awareness of bodily sensations, allowing you to better understand your body's demands and signals.

EMLIK. SAHRA

Somatic Healing for Beginners

tension Reduction: Somatic movements can reduce tension and anxiety by instilling a sense of serenity and relaxation.

Empowerment: By exploring movement on your own terms, you recover control of your body and emotions, fostering a sense of empowerment and self-discovery.

Incorporating Somatic Movements in Your Routine

Set aside time each week to experiment with somatic motions in order to incorporate them into your daily routine. You can also incorporate small exercise breaks throughout the day, particularly when you feel tension or worry building.

5.3 Dance as a Healing Tool.

What is Dance's Role as a Healing Tool?

Dance is a powerful means of self-expression and healing that goes beyond words. Dance allows you to connect with your body, release emotions, and cultivate joy. It is a comprehensive practice that promotes physical, emotional, and spiritual well-being, making it an excellent method for somatic healing.

How to Use Dance for Healing

Somatic Healing for Beginners

Find Your Space: Select a comfortable and safe area where you can dance freely. This might be the living room, a dance studio, or even outside.

Create a Playlist: Choose music that speaks to you. This could be uplifting, relaxing, or anything that motivates you to move. Allow yourself to become lost in the rhythm.

Warm Up: Before you begin dancing, gently stretch your body and take deep breaths. This prepares you for exercise and relieves any tension.

Let Go of Inhibition: When you start dancing, let go of any self-consciousness or judgment. Allow your body to move in whatever way that feels pleasant. Trust your instincts and follow the music.

Explore Movement: Experiment with various dancing styles, ranging from freeform and improvisational to regimented. Allow yourself to explore and express your feelings via movement.

Focus on Sensation: As you dance, notice how your body feels. Observe the sensations, emotions, and energies that pass through you. Allow yourself to be completely present in the event.

Dance can be an effective means of emotional release. Allow your movements to represent your emotions, whether they are grief, joy, or something else. There are no wrong motions; embrace your freedom of speech.

EMLIK. SAHRA

Somatic Healing for Beginners

End with Stillness: After dancing, take a time to sit or lie down in stillness. Think about the event and observe any changes in your body or emotions. Allow yourself to absorb the energy of the dance.

Benefits of Dance as a Healing Tool:

Incorporating dancing into your therapeutic path can give numerous benefits.

Emotional Expression: Dance allows you to express emotions that are difficult to verbalize, which promotes emotional healing.

Physical Health: Dancing is a form of exercise that can help with cardiovascular health, strength, and flexibility.

Dance releases endorphins, which promote emotions of happiness and well-being.

Dance promotes a deeper connection with your body, which aids in the development of self-acceptance and love.

Incorporating Dance in Your Routine

To make dance a regular part of your life, consider scheduling a weekly dance session. You may also incorporate spontaneous dancing breaks into your day—turn on your favorite music and move freely!

Movement techniques are critical components of somatic healing because they provide a mechanism to release tension, stress, and anxiety. Gentle Stretching

EMLIK. SAHRA

Somatic Healing for Beginners

Routines, Somatic Movements for Release, and Dance as a Healing Tool can help you reconnect with your body and build emotional resilience.

EMLIK. SAHRA

(Chapter 6:)

Tension-Release Techniques

Tension is a normal reaction to stress, trauma, and the rapid pace of modern life. When it builds in our bodies, it can cause discomfort, worry, and a loss of self-awareness. In this chapter, we'll look at three excellent tension-release techniques: Progressive Muscle Relaxation, EFT Tapping Basics, and Shaking for Stress Relief. These techniques help you release stress and reconnect with your body, resulting in a stronger sensation of serenity and well-being.

6.1 Progressive Muscle Relaxation.

What is Progressive Muscle Relaxation?

Progressive Muscle Relaxation (PMR) is a technique for systematically tensing and then releasing various muscle groups in the body. This practice, created by Dr. Edmund Jacobson in the early twentieth century, promotes profound relaxation and helps people become more aware of physical sensations linked with tension and relaxation. PMR fosters a deep sensation of calm by emphasizing the difference between tension and relaxation.

How To Practice Progressive Muscle Relaxation

Create a Calm Environment: Locate a peaceful, comfortable area where you will not be bothered. Sit or lie in a relaxed stance.

Take a few deep breaths, slowly inhaling with your nose and expelling through your mouth. Allow your body to relax while focusing on your breath.

Begin by focusing on your feet. Inhale deeply, then strain the muscles in your feet for roughly five seconds. Take note of the sensation of tension. Then exhale to completely relieve the tension. Pay attention to the differences in sensation.

Move Up the Body: Repeat this method with the following muscle groups: calves, thighs, abdomen, hands, arms, shoulders, neck, and face. For every area:

Inhale and strain your muscles for five seconds.
Exhale and let your body relax.
Focus on Relaxation: After you've worked through all of the muscle groups, take a time to notice how your body feels. Allow yourself to sink further into relaxation, focusing on feelings of serenity and tranquility.

Conclude the Practice: When you're ready, gradually return your focus to your surroundings. Wiggle your fingers and toes, take a few more deep breaths, then softly open your eyes.

Benefits of Progressive Muscle Relaxation:

EMLIK. SAHRA

Somatic Healing for Beginners

Practicing PMR provides a variety of benefits:

Reduced Stress and Anxiety: PMR reduces stress hormones and improves relaxation, which helps to alleviate anxiety.

Increased Body Awareness: This technique heightens your awareness of physical sensations, allowing you to identify tension and stress in your body.

Improved Sleep: Regular practice might aid with sleep quality by encouraging calm before bedtime.

PMR can increase emotional well-being, promoting a sense of serenity and happiness.

Integrating PMR Into Your Routine

To get the most out of Progressive Muscle Relaxation, incorporate it into your everyday routine. PMR can be practiced at the beginning or end of the day, or whenever you sense tension mounting. Even a few minutes can significantly improve your general well-being.

6.2 EFT Tapping Basics
What is EFT Tapping?

Emotional Freedom Techniques (EFT), sometimes known as tapping, is a therapy strategy that incorporates both cognitive and physical components. It entails tapping precise acupressure sites while focusing on emotional suffering, resulting in a potent avenue for healing and tension relief. EFT has grown in popularity due to its ease of use and effectiveness in dealing with a variety of emotional and physical difficulties.

How to Practice EFT Tapping.

Identify Your Issue: Start by identifying the issue or emotion you want to address. This could include anxiety, panic, or physical discomfort.

Rate Your Intensity: On a scale of 0 to 10, rate the severity of your problem. This will allow you to monitor your progress throughout the practice.

Create a setup statement that admits your problem while affirming self-acceptance. Like the following: "Even though I feel anxious about [specific situation], I deeply and completely accept myself."

Tapping Sequence:

Begin tapping on the Karate Chop point (the outer edge of your hand) and repeat your setup phrase three times.
Then, continue through the following tapping points while using a reminder word linked to your problem:
Eyebrow Point
Side of the eye.
Under the eye
Under the nose.
Chin Point

Somatic Healing for Beginners

Collarbone Point.

Under the arm.

Top of the head.

Take a Deep Breath: Once you've completed the tapping process, take a deep breath and check in with yourself. Rerate the severity of your problem on a scale of 0 to 10. Observe any changes in your emotions or experiences.

Repeat as needed: If the intensity remains strong, continue tapping until you notice a decrease in the emotional energy linked with the situation.

Benefits of EFT Tapping:

EFT tapping provides several benefits:

Emotional Release: Tapping helps you process and release pent-up emotions, which promotes emotional healing.

Reduced Stress and Anxiety: Many people report that tapping efficiently relieves anxiety and stress, resulting in a greater sense of peace.

Increased Clarity: EFT removes emotional barriers, resulting in greater mental clarity and focus.

Tapping takes a holistic approach to healing by addressing both the emotional and physical components of suffering.

Incorporating EFT Tapping into your routine

EFT tapping can be used as needed or integrated into your regular routine. You might use it in the morning to establish a pleasant tone for the day, or in the evening to relax and release the day's burdens.

6.3 Shaking to relieve stress

What Does Shaking Mean for Stress Relief?

Shaking is a simple but effective technique for relieving tension and stress from the body. Inspired by animal behavior, this technique helps you shrug off tension and promotes relaxation and renewal. Shaking involves the entire body, promoting a feeling of lightness and freedom.

How to Practice Shaking for Stress Relief.

Find Your Space: Select a safe and comfortable environment in which you can shake freely without restraint.

Stand comfortably with your feet parallel and hip-width apart. Allow your knees to bend slightly for further support.

Begin by taking a few deep breaths to center yourself. Inhale deeply through your nose and exhale through your mouth to let your body relax.

Somatic Healing for Beginners

Begin shaking your hands, arms, and legs softly. Allow the exercise to intensify as your body moves naturally. You can shake your entire body or just the places where you feel tightness.

Embrace Your Movement: Let your movements be spontaneous. Remove any tension or stress by encouraging laughter or vocal expression if it feels appropriate.

Continue for Several Minutes: Shake for a few minutes, gradually increasing the intensity before tapering down. Listen to your body and quit when it feels appropriate.

Finish with Stillness: After shaking, come to a stop. Take a deep breath and note how your body feels. Appreciate the feelings of lightness and relaxation.

Benefits of Shaking for Stress Relief:

Incorporating shaking into your self-care practice can result in a variety of benefits:

Tension Release: Shaking effectively relieves physical and emotional tension and promotes relaxation.

Mood Enhancement: Shaking's spontaneous nature can elevate your mood and encourage sentiments of joy and freedom.

EMLIK. SAHRA

Somatic Healing for Beginners

Increased Energy: This practice can rejuvenate your body, leaving you feeling energized and renewed.

Mind-Body Connection: Shaking helps you connect with your body and its natural instincts, resulting in a deeper sense of awareness and present.

Integrating Shaking into Your Routine

Shaking can be done whenever you feel tension building up, whether during a break at work, after a tough day, or as part of your daily routine. Consider devoting a few minutes per day to this freeing activity.

Tension release techniques are essential components of somatic healing, allowing you to let go of tension, trauma, and anxiety. Progressive Muscle Relaxation, EFT Tapping, and Shaking for Stress Relief can help you relax and reconnect with your body.

(Chapter 7:)

Mindfulness and Meditation.

In a world that can feel chaotic and stressful, mindfulness and meditation techniques provide a safe haven. These methods allow us to return to the present moment, increase awareness, and build inner calm. This chapter delves into three strong aspects of mindfulness and meditation: mindful awareness practices, guided meditations for healing, and gratitude journaling. By implementing these practices into your everyday routine, you can foster a stronger connection with yourself and encourage healing in your life.

7.1 Mindful Awareness Practices.

What is Mindful Awareness?

Mindful awareness is the practice of remaining completely present and involved in the moment without passing judgment. It entails paying attention to our ideas, feelings, and physiological experiences with curiosity and openness. This practice can be used in any area of life, transforming ordinary tasks into opportunities for connection and insight.

How to cultivate mindful awareness.

Somatic Healing for Beginners

Mindful Breathing: Take a few deep breaths. Concentrate on the sensation of the breath entering and exiting your body. Observe how your chest and abdomen rise and fall. If your mind wanders, softly return your focus to your breathing.

thoughtful Eating: Make meals a thoughtful experience. Sit in a calm area free of distractions. Take a moment to notice your food's colors, textures, and scents. Chew gently and relish every bite. Take note of the flavors and how your body feels while you nurture it.

Mindful Walking: Go for a walk in a calm environment, whether indoors or outside. Pay attention to the sensations in your body as you move: the feel of your feet on the ground, the rhythm of your breathing, and the sights and sounds around you. Let go of any destination and just enjoy the experience of walking.

Body Scan: Lie down comfortably and close your eyes. Beginning with your toes, bring your awareness to each part of your body, noting any sensations without judgment. Allow yourself to relax and relieve tension in each place. This exercise promotes a stronger connection to your body and a sense of grounding.

Set reminders throughout the day to halt and practice mindful awareness. These can be as easy as taking a few deep breaths or paying close attention to your surroundings. Make a habit of returning your focus to the current moment.

Benefits of Mindful Awareness Practices

EMLIK. SAHRA

Incorporating mindful awareness into your life can produce numerous benefits:

Reduced Stress and Anxiety: Mindfulness allows you to observe your thoughts and emotions without becoming involved in them, which alleviates feelings of overload.

Enhanced Emotional Regulation: By becoming more aware of your emotional reactions, you can build resilience and respond to difficulties with clarity and calm.

Improved Focus and Concentration: Mindfulness improves your capacity to focus on tasks and cognitive performance, making it easier to manage everyday duties.

Greater Connection to the Present: Mindfulness encourages a deeper appreciation for life as it unfolds, which improves your overall sense of well-being.

7.2 Guided Meditations for Healing

What are Guided Meditations?

Guided meditations involve listening to a facilitator who guides you through a meditative experience that frequently incorporates imagery and relaxation techniques. These meditations can help you achieve deeper levels of awareness, facilitate healing, and build a sense of serenity.

How to Practice Guided Meditations:

Create a Calm Environment: Locate a quiet area where you can sit or lie comfortably. Consider dimming the lights or lighting a candle to create a relaxing mood.

Choose Your Meditation: There are a variety of guided meditations available online or via meditation apps. You may choose one that focuses on healing, stress reduction, or self-compassion.

Close your eyes and take some deep breaths. Allow your body to relax before entering the meditation space.

Listen to the facilitator's voice and allow yourself to be guided through the meditation. Visualize the imagery and concentrate on your breathing, sensations, and emotions as they arise.

Integrate the Experience: After the meditation, take a minute to reflect on your experiences. Take note of how your body feels and any insights that emerge during the practice.

Advantages of Guided Meditations for Healing

Guided meditations can offer a variety of advantages, including:

Somatic Healing for Beginners

Deep Relaxation: These meditations frequently promote profound relaxation, which helps to alleviate tension and anxiety.

Enhanced Self-Compassion: Many guided meditations emphasize self-love and compassion, which fosters a healthy relationship with oneself.

Emotional Processing: Guided meditations can help you process and release emotions, which promotes healing from prior trauma.

Guided meditations can help you connect with your inner knowledge and intuition by using visualization and introspection to guide your healing path.

Incorporating Guided Meditations into your Routine

Aim to practice guided meditations on a regular basis—daily, weekly, or as needed. Set out a definite period each day, such as the morning or evening, to establish a consistent practice that benefits your mind and spirit.

7.3 Gratitude journaling

What is Gratitude Journaling?

Gratitude journaling entails routinely writing down what you are grateful for. This exercise promotes a positive outlook and helps turn your attention away from what is lacking in your life and toward the abundance that is already

Somatic Healing for Beginners

available. Practicing thankfulness can help you build resilience and emotional well-being.

How to Start a Gratitude Journal

Choose Your Journal: Select a notebook or digital platform that appeals to you. The act of writing by hand can improve the experience, but digital choices are also viable.

Set a regular time for your thankfulness journaling practice. Whether it's first thing in the morning or before bed, consistency is essential.

Begin by jotting down three things you are grateful for every day. These can be large or tiny, ranging from the beauty of nature to a thoughtful gesture from a friend.

Reflect on Why You're glad: After you've listed your three objects, take a moment to consider why you're glad for each. Consider how they affect your life and add to your pleasure.

Include Positive Affirmations: Along with your gratitude list, try writing positive affirmations that speak to you. This can help to reinforce a good outlook.

Review and Reflect: Keep a thankfulness notebook and revisit it on a regular basis. Reflecting on earlier entries might help you identify patterns of appreciation and strengthen your thankfulness practice.

Somatic Healing for Beginners

Benefits of Gratitude Journaling:

Journaling your appreciation provides various benefits:

Increased Happiness: Research indicates that gratitude writing might improve overall happiness and life satisfaction.

Reduced tension: Concentrating on the positive aspects of your life can help relieve tension and anxiety, forming a barrier against negativity.

Enhanced Relationships: Practicing thankfulness can help you build stronger relationships with others by encouraging kindness and appreciation.

Greater Resilience: Acknowledging the good in your life will help you build resilience and face problems with a more cheerful attitude.

Incorporating Gratitude Journaling into Your Life

Make thankfulness journaling an important part of your everyday practice. Over time, you may notice that it shifts your viewpoint, allowing you to recognize beauty and wealth in daily situations.
Mindfulness and meditation are important activities that can improve your overall well-being. By combining mindful awareness, guided meditations, and gratitude journaling into your daily routine, you can develop a stronger connection with yourself, support healing, and build inner peace.

EMLIK. SAHRA

(Chapter 8:)

Creative Expression.

Creative expression is a powerful healing tool that allows us to process emotions, relieve stress, and reconnect with our true selves. This chapter delves into three transforming kinds of creative expression: art therapy basics, writing for healing, and music and sound healing. Engaging in these techniques allows you to tap into creativity's intrinsic healing potential, opening up new avenues for emotional release and personal growth.

8.1 Art Therapy Basics

What is art therapy?

Art therapy is a therapeutic approach that uses the creative process of making art to promote mental, emotional, and physical health. It is founded on the idea that artistic expression can help people process events and feelings that are difficult to convey in words. Art therapy promotes self-discovery and healing via a variety of artistic techniques, including painting, sketching, sculpting, and collage.

How Does Art Therapy Work?

Somatic Healing for Beginners

The Therapeutic Relationship: In art therapy, a qualified art therapist leads people through the creative process. This secure and supportive setting promotes open expression and exploration of emotions.

Nonverbal Expression: Art therapy allows for nonverbal communication, making it very beneficial for people who struggle to express their emotions. Making art can help you overcome cognitive hurdles and gain deeper emotional insights.

Process Over Product: In art therapy, the emphasis is on the process of creation rather than the end result. This encourages people to let go of their perfectionism and accept spontaneity, resulting in a sense of freedom and discovery.

Symbolic Representation: Art can be used to symbolize thoughts and feelings, creating a visual language for experiences that are overpowering or difficult to explain.

Getting started with art therapy

Gather Your Materials: You do not need sophisticated supplies to participate in art therapy. Gather simple supplies like paper, colored pencils, paint, and clay.

Set Aside Time: Schedule a dedicated time for your creative activity. This might be as little as 15 minutes per day or longer if you're feeling inspired.

EMLIK. SAHRA

Somatic Healing for Beginners

Create a Safe Space: Locate a quiet, comfortable area where you can work without distractions. This place should be inviting and allow you to fully immerse yourself in the process.

Begin by checking in with your emotions. How are you feeling today? Allow these emotions to influence your creative expression. You might choose colors, shapes, or forms that correspond to your emotional condition.

Let go of Expectations: Accept the freedom to create without judgment. Allow your artwork to take shape naturally, without the necessity for it to look a certain way.

Benefits of Art Therapy

Art therapy provides several benefits, including:

Emotional Release: Creative expression can help to release pent-up emotions, reducing anxiety and stress.

Enhanced Self-Awareness: The creative process frequently provides individuals with insights into their thoughts and feelings, leading to increased self-awareness.

Improved Communication: Art can act as a bridge for communication, allowing people to communicate emotions that are difficult to express verbally.

Somatic Healing for Beginners

A Sense of success: Finishing a creative activity can give you a sense of success and increase your self-esteem, which reinforces positive sentiments about yourself.

8.2 Writing for Healing.

Writing: Its Therapeutic Potential

Writing has long been acknowledged as an effective technique for introspection and healing. Journaling, poetry, and storytelling allow people to explore their thoughts and feelings while also obtaining clarity and understanding. Writing for healing allows you to express your emotions, alleviate stress, and gain a better understanding of yourself.

How to Start Writing for Healing

Choose Your Medium: Determine how you want to express yourself. Journaling, poetry, creative writing, and even letters to yourself or others are all viable options.

Set some time for your writing exercise. This might be a daily habit or a weekly commitment, depending on your availability.

Find Your Space: Select a comfortable and quiet location where you will be motivated to write. This could be at a desk, in a comfortable chair, or even outside in nature.

Somatic Healing for Beginners

Write freely: Allow oneself to write without being censored. Set a timer for 10-15 minutes and allow your thoughts to flow across the page. Don't worry about grammar, punctuation, or consistency; just write what comes to mind.

Explore Your Emotions: Write about your feelings. Ask yourself thoughtful questions: How am I feeling right now? What experiences shaped my emotions? Allow your writing to reflect your inner world.

Incorporate Prompts: If you're feeling stuck, use writing prompts to spark your imagination. Prompts could include questions like "What does healing look like for me?"" or "Describe a joyful moment in my life."

Benefits of Writing for Healing:

Writing for healing can provide a wide range of advantages, including:

Emotional Clarity: Writing out your thoughts and feelings might help you achieve better emotional clarity and understanding.

Catharsis: Writing can be a cathartic outlet for painful feelings and experiences.

Personal Growth: Writing promotes introspection and self-reflection, resulting in personal growth and resilience.

Connection to Self: Writing allows you to reconnect with your inner self while exploring your values, objectives, and goals.

EMLIK. SAHRA

8.3 Music and Sound Healing.

The Healing Power of Music and Sound.

Music and music have a powerful influence on our emotions and well-being. Sound can help with relaxation, emotional release, and healing, whether you listen to music, play an instrument, or engage in sound healing techniques. Sound therapy uses diverse frequencies, rhythms, and vibrations to facilitate healing on the physical, emotional, and spiritual levels.

How to Bring Music and Sound Healing into Your Life

Create Playlists: Choose playlists that reflect your emotional state. Choose tunes that inspire you, comfort your soul, or bring back memories.

Sound baths entail immersing yourself in healing sounds produced by instruments such as singing bowls, gongs, and chimes. These sessions induce profound relaxation and can be attended in person or via recorded sessions.

Explore Music Creation: If you enjoy playing an instrument or singing, you can use music to communicate your emotions. You don't need to be a professional musician to benefit from playing for yourself.

Somatic Healing for Beginners

Mindful Listening: Immerse yourself completely in the experience of music. Close your eyes, take a deep breath, and focus on the sensations created by the sound.

Chanting and reciting mantras can induce a meditative state and aid in emotional recovery. Choose affirmations or mantras that are meaningful to you and repeat them aloud or silently.

Benefits of Music and Sound Healing

Engaging with music and sound provides a variety of healing effects.

Emotional Regulation: Music has the ability to evoke and regulate emotions, hence reducing tension and anxiety.

Enhanced Relaxation: Listening to relaxing music or practicing sound therapy might help you relax and lower your heart rate and blood pressure.

Connection to the Present: Music can help you stay in the present moment, providing a break from racing thoughts and worries.

Creativity and Self-Expression: Music encourages creativity and self-expression, allowing you to explore your emotions in new ways.
Creative expression is an essential part of the somatic healing process, providing numerous avenues for emotional release, self-discovery, and personal development. Art therapy, writing for healing, and music and sound

healing can all help you tap into the transformational power of creativity and illuminate your road to wholeness.

(Chapter 9:)

Daily Rituals for Healing

Establishing regular rituals is one of the most effective methods to lay the groundwork for somatic healing. These rituals not only anchor you in the present moment but also act as effective tools for self-care and emotional management. In this chapter, we will discuss morning routines to start your day with intention, evening wind-down techniques to create relaxation, and how to smoothly incorporate healing into your daily life. Integrating these rituals into your daily routine can help you achieve a deeper feeling of well-being, reduce stress, and build resilience.

9.1 Morning Routines for Starting Your Day

The way you begin your day sets the tone for the hours that follow. A mindful morning ritual can help you achieve greater attention, clarity, and positivity. Incorporating somatic techniques into your morning routine creates a holy place for self-care and intention-setting.

Creating Your Morning Ritual

Somatic Healing for Beginners

Wake Up Mindfully: Start the day with a calm wakeup. Instead of reaching for your phone, stretch in bed. Wiggle your fingers and toes, take a deep breath, and pay attention to the sensations in your body. This simple act of mindfulness can provide a sense of comfort and connection.

Hydrate: After a good night's sleep, your body desires water. Start your morning with a glass of water. You can improve the experience by adding lemon or fresh herbs, which will awaken your senses and provide a pleasant start.

Diaphragmatic Breathing: Use a few minutes of diaphragmatic breathing to ground oneself. Sit comfortably, close your eyes, and rest one hand on your heart and the other on your stomach. Inhale deeply through your nose, letting your stomach expand. Feel the tension release as you exhale slowly through your mouth. Repeat for a few breaths, paying attention to your body's sensations.

Set Intentions: Take a time to consider what you want to achieve in your day. To reinforce your commitment, write your intentions in a notebook or speak them loudly. For example, "I will embrace joy" or "I will approach challenges with calmness."

Gentle Movement: To awaken your body, stretch or practice yoga. Concentrate on actions that feel pleasant, letting your body direct you. This could include neck rolls, shoulder shrugs, and a couple sun salutations. Movement in the morning helps to relieve sleep-related tension and prepares you for the day.

Somatic Healing for Beginners

Mindful Breakfast: Eat a balanced breakfast mindfully. Enjoy every bite, paying close attention to the flavors and sensations. Consider include items that will fuel your body, such as fruits, entire grains, and protein sources. Eating mindfully can help you connect with your body and develop a sense of gratitude.

thanks Practice: Before starting your day, take a moment to express thanks. Consider three things for which you are grateful, no matter how large or small. This simple technique can help you adopt a more positive and resilient mindset.

By creating a morning routine that speaks to you, you create a powerful intention for the day. Remember that the goal is to tailor these routines to your specific needs, allowing your intuition to guide you in what feels right for your body and spirit.

9.2 Evening Wind-Down Practices

As the day draws to a close, developing a tranquil nighttime wind-down ritual is critical for transitioning from the hectic pace of daily living to restful sleep. These techniques assist release the day's stress, allowing you to relax and regain balance.

Designing Your Evening Ritual.

Digital Detox: Start your wind-down by turning off all devices at least an hour before bedtime. Blue light from devices can impair your ability to fall asleep. Instead, choose relaxing activities such as reading or writing.

EMLIK. SAHRA

To create a relaxing atmosphere, dim the lights in your home and consider lighting candles or utilizing essential scents. Scents such as lavender, chamomile, or sandalwood might help you relax and prepare for sleep.

Gentle stretching or restorative yoga can help relieve tension that has built up over the day. Choose postures that promote relaxation, such as Child's Pose, Legs Up the Wall, or Supta Baddha Konasana (Reclined Bound Angle Pose).

Mindful Reflection: Set aside a few minutes to reflect on your day. What was deemed successful? What difficulties did you face? Consider writing your thoughts in a journal to help you process emotions and find clarity.

Guided Meditation: Add a guided meditation to your evening routine. Find a meditation that speaks to you, whether it is about relaxation, gratitude, or stress reduction. Allow the calming voice and imagery to lead you to a peaceful state of mind.

Breathing Exercises: End your evening with long, relaxing breaths. Practice the 4-7-8 breathing technique: inhale through your nose for 4, hold for 7, and exhale through your mouth for 8. Repeat this cycle multiple times to help your body relax and remove tension.

Make a Sleep Sanctuary: Prepare your sleeping environment to promote restful sleep. Ensure that your bedroom is dark, quiet, and cool. Consider utilizing blackout curtains, white noise generators, or sleep masks to create the best sleeping environment.

Gratitude Journaling: Before falling asleep, take a moment to write down three things you loved about your day. This exercise promotes contentment and allows you to finish the day on a pleasant note.

Establishing a soothing nightly wind-down regimen allows your body and mind to smoothly transition into rest. This not only enhances the quality of your sleep, but it also promotes a more relaxed and peaceful state of mind.

9.3 Integrating Healing into Daily Life

Incorporating somatic healing activities into your regular routine does not have to be daunting. Small, deliberate acts can lead to major improvements in your emotional and physical well-being. Here are some techniques for easily incorporating healing practices into your daily routine.

Everyday Healing Practices.

Mindful Moments: Throughout the day, take periodic breaks to check in with your body and breath. Pause for a few seconds and take a deep breath while stretching your arms aloft or rotating your shoulders. This easy practice might help you relax and focus on the present moment.

Movement Breaks: If you have a sedentary work or spend a lot of time sitting, arrange regular movement breaks. Stand up, stretch, or go for a brief walk to refresh your body and mind. Even a minute or two can boost your energy and focus.

Nature Connection: Whenever feasible, include nature into your daily life. Take your breaks outside, go for a walk in the park, or simply relax in your own lawn. Nature provides a grounding effect, which reduces stress and improves your sense of wellbeing.

Mindful Eating: Eat mindfully during meals. Slow down and enjoy each bite, paying close attention to the flavors and textures of your food. This exercise promotes a stronger connection with your body and increases your appreciation of nutritious food.

Affirmations and mantras: Use positive affirmations in your daily life. Choose phrases that speak to you, such as "I am capable" or "I embrace joy." Repeat these affirmations throughout the day to reinforce positive thoughts and increase self-confidence.

Short Meditation Sessions: Even a few minutes of meditation can yield major results. Consider taking 5-10 minutes during your lunch break or before bedtime for a small meditation practice. Apps and internet tools provide guided meditations to help you focus and center yourself.

Journaling as an everyday Practice: Try incorporating journaling into your everyday routine. You may opt to write in the morning to set intentions, or in the evening to reflect on your day. Journaling can help you process emotions, track your recovery progress, and increase your self-awareness.

Expressive Movement: Incorporate spontaneous movement into your daily activities. Whether you're dancing in your kitchen, taking a mindful walk, or doing yoga during a break, expressive movement allows you to connect with your body and release tension.

Check in with Yourself: Set reminders throughout the day to pause and reflect on your emotions and physical sensations. Ask yourself how you're feeling, both mentally and physically. This technique increases self-awareness and encourages you to respect your own needs.

Creating daily healing rituals is a transforming practice that allows you to grow mindfulness, reduce stress, and build emotional resilience. By establishing focused morning and evening routines and incorporating healing practices into your daily life, you can provide a supportive framework for your somatic healing process.

Remember, the goal is to approach these rituals with curiosity and openness. Allow yourself to try with various methods to discover what works best for you. As you embark on this path, recognize the potential of routine to improve your well-being, strengthen your connection to your body, and develop a life of healing and joy.

(Chapter 10:)

Establishing a Support System

A strong support system is critical in the journey of somatic recovery. While self-care techniques are important, the relationships we form with others can greatly aid in our recovery journey. This chapter will go over how to locate community and support, know when to seek professional help, and develop self-compassion and patience along the journey. Together, these ingredients form a supportive environment that allows you to thrive.

10.1 Find Community and Support

Finding your tribe is vital for emotional and psychological recovery. A supportive group offers a sense of connection, shared experiences, and encouragement as you embark on your somatic healing path.

Exploring Community Options

Local Support Groups: Many communities have support groups that focus on mental health, trauma, or specialized healing techniques. Look for groups that share your journey, whether they are focused on somatic healing, trauma recovery, or overall wellness. These groups frequently provide safe locations in which to share experiences, learn from others, and seek help.

internet Communities: In this digital age, internet platforms provide numerous options to engage with others. Websites, forums, and social media groups focused on physical healing, mental health, or personal development can be quite beneficial. Seek out communities that share your ideals, and don't be afraid to introduce yourself. Engaging with others electronically might help you feel more connected, especially if you live in a remote region.

Workshops and Retreats: Attending workshops or retreats centered on somatic practices can be an effective method to meet like-minded people. These immersive experiences not only help you comprehend somatic healing, but they also allow you to connect with others who are on the same journey. The common experience of engaging in therapeutic activities fosters a link that might continue long after the event is over.

Many community organizations, yoga studios, and wellness centers provide classes in mindfulness, yoga, and other somatic practices. Attending these sessions on a regular basis allows you to meet others in your community who have similar interests. Consider enrolling in a course that allows you to learn and grow with others, building a sense of community.

Friends and family: Do not underestimate the value of your current relationships. Share your adventure with friends and family who are encouraging and understanding. Open interactions can strengthen connections and foster an environment in which you feel comfortable expressing your healing experience.

Finding a Mentor: A mentor or guide can provide significant insights and encouragement as you embark on your somatic healing path. Look for someone who understands you—this could be a teacher, therapist, or more experienced peer. Their advice can make you feel safer about your journey by presenting you with a plethora of expertise and experiences.

Developing Connection

Active Engagement: Do not wait for community members to contact you. Take the initiative and engage with others. Attend meetings, contribute to debates, and share your experiences. Active participation builds connections and encourages others to open up.

Be Vulnerable: Vulnerability is an essential ingredient in developing authentic connections. Sharing your struggles and triumphs allows others to relate to your situation, fostering a safe environment for mutual support. Remember that vulnerability is a strength that promotes deeper ties.

When communicating with others in your support community, use active listening. When someone shares their experience, pay close attention and reply with empathy and understanding. This approach not only develops relationships, but it also fosters an environment of support.

Somatic Healing for Beginners

Celebrate Others: Take time to recognize the accomplishments of others in your community. Recognizing their accomplishments builds a sense of belonging and strengthens the supportive environment you seek. This technique can lead to a positive feedback loop, encouraging everyone to thrive.

Finding a supporting community is an important part of somatic recovery. As you interact with others, you'll discover that shared experiences can lighten the load on your journey and inspire you to embrace healing wholeheartedly.

10.2 When Should You Seek Professional Help?

While developing a support system is extremely beneficial, there are instances when professional assistance is required. Recognizing when to seek help is critical to your healing path. Professional therapists, counselors, and other practitioners contribute knowledge and techniques to assist you traverse difficult emotional landscapes.

When to Seek Professional Help

Persistent Symptoms: If your trauma, anxiety, or tension symptoms remain despite your best self-care attempts, it may be time to seek professional treatment. Expert counsel can help with symptoms such as chronic anxiety, sleeplessness, and emotional dysregulation.

Somatic Healing for Beginners

Feeling Overwhelmed: If your emotions are overpowering or uncontrolled, reaching out to a mental health professional can help. Therapists can provide coping skills and assistance targeted to your specific requirements.

Traumatic Experiences: If you have been through substantial trauma, such as loss, abuse, or a serious disease, consulting with a therapist skilled in trauma-informed approaches can help you process it safely.

Relationship Difficulties: If you struggle to form healthy relationships or are frequently lonely, a therapist can assist you in addressing underlying issues and developing better communication skills.

Seeking Deeper Understanding: If you want to improve your self-awareness and understanding of your emotional patterns, a professional can guide you through this process, allowing you to uncover insights that would be difficult to discover on your own.

Integrating Somatic Practices: If you want to incorporate somatic practices into your recovery plan but are unsure how to do so, consult with a somatic therapy expert. They can assist you in tailoring techniques to your specific needs and providing support as you navigate your journey.

Finding the Right Professional.

Credentials: When looking for a mental health expert, consider their qualifications and areas of focus. Look for a practitioner who specializes in somatic therapy, trauma rehabilitation, or anxiety management.

EMLIK. SAHRA

appointments: Many therapists provide first appointments, which can help you assess whether their method is compatible with your goals. Use this opportunity to inquire about their methodology and expertise with somatic practices.

Trust Your Intuition: The therapeutic connection is based on trust. When meeting with a potential therapist, trust your instincts. If you feel at ease and understood, it's likely that you've found the right person.

Be Open to Change: If your first session with a therapist does not feel right, don't be afraid to look for someone else. The right therapeutic relationship is essential for healing, and you should seek out a professional with whom you feel comfortable.

10.3 Self-compassion and Patience.

Self-compassion and patience are essential skills to develop as you embark on your healing journey. Healing is not a linear process; it frequently involves ups and downs. Practicing self-compassion enables you to approach problems with kindness and understanding.

How to cultivate self-compassion

Somatic Healing for Beginners

Accept Your Journey: Recognize that recovery is a process, not a destination. Recognize your accomplishments, no matter how small they may be. Recognize every accomplishment you make and don't underestimate your progress.

Practice Self-Soothing: When confronted with difficult emotions or disappointments, use self-soothing strategies. This could include deep breathing, moderate movement, or engaging in activities that bring you joy. You should treat yourself with the same kindness that you would extend to a friend in need.

Develop a Positive Inner Dialogue: Pay attention to what's going on in your mind. Challenge your negative self-talk and replace it with positive ones. "I am doing my best, and healing takes time," is a more appropriate statement than "I should be over this by now."

Accept Imperfections: Recognize that flaws are a normal part of being human. Allow oneself to feel a spectrum of emotions without judgment. Accept that it's acceptable to not have everything figured out and that your journey is uniquely yours.

Practicing Patience

Be reasonable in your expectations: recovery takes time. Be reasonable with yourself and accept that improvement might come gradually. Stay away from comparing your path to others' and concentrate on your own.

EMLIK. SAHRA

Somatic Healing for Beginners

Accept the Process: Give the healing process your full attention rather than racing to the finish line. Acknowledge the feelings that come up and accept them as necessary phases in your journey. Every experience, especially the difficult ones, helps you grow.

Establish a Space for Reflection: Make time every day for introspection. You can digest your experiences and obtain understanding of your healing path by journaling, practicing meditation, or just spending time alone yourself.

Rely on Your Support Network: Rely on your network for assistance when facing difficult circumstances. Speak with loved ones, neighbors, or other community members who can offer support and empathy. Emotional burdens might be lessened by talking about your feelings.

Celebrate Little Wins: Along the journey, recognize and commemorate your little successes. Every accomplishment is deserving of praise, whether it's finishing a meditation routine or making a connection with a helpful group of people.

Creating a network of support is crucial to your somatic healing process. By establishing a supportive network, knowing when to get expert assistance, and exercising patience and self-compassion, you foster an atmosphere that supports your development.

In summary

It's time to take stock of your journey through somatic healing as you approach its conclusion, acknowledge the knowledge you've acquired, and look forward to the exciting opportunities that lie ahead. Maintaining your physical and mental well-being throughout your life is a sign of your dedication to overall heath, as healing is a continuous process. We'll consider your journey, discuss the next steps for your practice, and provide support for ongoing development in this conclusion.

Considering Your Journey Again

Stop for a moment and consider where you started. Maybe you picked up this book to help you deal with stress, worry, or the burden of past experiences. Maybe you were brought in by curiosity about somatic healing and its potential to alter your life. No matter where you begin, recognize the bravery required to begin this journey.

You have encountered a wide range of techniques over the course of the chapters, all aimed at enabling you to reestablish a connection with your body and let go of burdens that no longer serve you. You've developed a toolkit of tactics to deal with life's obstacles, from movement routines and creative expression to breathing exercises and grounding exercises.

EMLIK. SAHRA

Somatic Healing for Beginners

Think back to the times when you were enlightened, the realizations that helped you on your road, and the little triumphs you've had along the route. Have you discovered a new breathing method that helps you to relax? Have you found a happy method to use dance or art to express yourself? By thinking back on these encounters, you can gain a deeper knowledge of your path and demonstrate the transformational potential of somatic practices.

Writing Down Your Experience

Think about writing in a journal about your experiences as you reflect. Jot down your feelings, ideas, and any significant breakthroughs. As you proceed with your healing process, this exercise can help you firmly establish your insights and provide a useful point of reference. Never forget that every action, no matter how tiny, advances your own development.

The Next Moves in Your Practice of Somatic Healing
After establishing a strong foundation in somatic healing, it's time to consider your next course of action. Healing is a continuous process rather than a final destination. Here are some suggestions to keep up your routine:

Establish a Daily Routine: You can improve your sense of wellbeing by including somatic practices into your daily routine. Pick a couple of practices that you find meaningful, such as a grounding exercise in the afternoon, an evening meditation, or an early breathing exercise. Consistency is crucial, and carving out only 15 minutes a day can reap big advantages.

Somatic Healing for Beginners

Establish Intentions: Make sure your practice has clear goals for each week or month. What aims do you have in mind? Whether your objective is to develop self-awareness, boost creativity, or lower anxiety, having clear intentions can help you stay motivated and focused.

Try New Methods: Don't be scared to investigate novel approaches and modalities. Somatic healing is a large and varied field. To find out what speaks to you the most, think about taking community classes, online courses, or workshops.

Continue to Be Curious: Maintain an interest in your body and mind. Observe how various strategies effect your physical and mental well-being. Keeping an open mind can help you connect more profoundly to your healing process.

Create a Supportive Network: Keep cultivating the relationships you've met along the road. Interact with your neighbors, whether they're friends, family, or other supporters. Talking about your experiences could speed up the healing process and give you support while you face hurdles.

Track Your Development: Maintain a healing journal to document your ideas, experiences, and advancements. You can notice trends and find areas for improvement by keeping a journal of your ideas. You'll gather a plethora of knowledge that can throw light on your route over time.

Integrate Mindfulness: Mindfulness is a powerful tool that helps somatic techniques. Incorporate mindfulness into your daily life by paying attention to your thoughts, feelings, and sensations. Having this understanding can help you deal with pressures more graciously and resiliently.

Seek Professional Assistance: If you wish to go deeper into a topic or encounter barriers that are too large for you to manage, don't be hesitant to seek professional help. A somatic-practices-focused therapist or counselor can offer advice tailored to your needs.

Investigate Further Learning: To improve your understanding of somatic healing, consider reading more books, attending workshops, or taking online courses. You'll be able to navigate your path more effectively as your knowledge grows.

Remain Adaptable: Because life is dynamic, your rehabilitation process will alter over time. Maintain adaptability and openness to change. What works for you now may not work for you in the future, which is fine.

Motivation for ongoing development.

As you move forward, adopt the mindset of a lifelong learner. Healing is a dynamic process, therefore there will be possibilities for growth as well as challenges to face. Keep in mind that physical and emotional health changes are normal. Allow yourself to express your emotions without passing judgment.

Self-Compassion Exercise: Continue to practice self-compassion throughout your trip. Honor your successes, no matter how modest, and treat yourself with the same kindness that you would show a good friend. Remember that healing takes time, and it's okay to face setbacks along the way. Every difficulty provides an opportunity for growth and education.

Recognize Your Strength: Be mindful of the courage required to participate in somatic healing. You are demonstrating bravery and resilience by prioritizing your health. You should be proud of the proactive attitude you are taking towards your rehabilitation.

Embrace Community: Surround yourself with positive, inspiring individuals who will inspire and motivate you. Tell them about your trip, and don't be hesitant to seek support and advise from your community. Making relationships will aid in your recovery and act as a continual reminder that you are not alone.

Stay Inspired: Continue to look for inspiration to feed your passion for healing. Sourcing books, attending courses, or listening to podcasts—never stop nurturing your curiosity and need for growth. Inspiration can help you gain new perspectives and fuel for your path.

Develop Gratitude: Recognize how to use thanksgiving as a growth approach. Consider your blessings on a regular basis, whether they be tiny pleasures in life, support you have received, or progress you have made. Practicing thankfulness may alter your perspective and improve your overall well-being.

Last Words

When you finish this book, take your newfound knowledge and habits with you. Somatic healing is a profound journey that includes reconnecting with your body, letting go of tension, and gaining a better sense of peace and wellbeing. Accept this trip with an open mind and heart.

You can grow, heal, and thrive. Have faith in your ability to face life's obstacles, and remember that every action you do indicates your resilience. May you find joy in the process and a sense of empowerment as you continue your somatic healing journey.

I am happy that you have let me walk this journey with you. I hope your path offers you progress, healing, and a deeper connection with yourself.
Somatic Healing.

EMLIK. SAHRA

Call to action

Appreciate you reading! I would want to take a moment to personally thank you for selecting to read my work. Your time and effort are much valued; perhaps, this book will give you insightful analysis and successful techniques.

Your comments are very much valued as I develop as an author. I would love to hear your thoughts—whether positive or constructive—so I can improve and make future works even more helpful and engaging.

 I respectfully ask that you write an honest review whether you thought this book was beneficial or if you could see anything improved. Your observations will not only help me but also guide other readers toward appropriate materials.

I appreciate your support once more; I am looking forward your comments. Good wishes,

EMLIK. SAHRA

www.ingramcontent.com/pod-product-compliance
Lightning Source LLC
Chambersburg PA
CBHW061722250726
48657CB00002B/731